To all those who work for justice,
everywhere —M.R.

For Claudia, with love and admiration —R.G.C.

 Published in the United States by Random House Studio,
an imprint of Random House Children's Books,
a division of Penguin Random House LLC, New York.
Random House Studio and the colophon are trademarks of Penguin Random House LLC.

Visit us on the Web! rhcbooks.com
Educators and librarians, for a variety of teaching tools, visit us at RHTeachersLibrarians.com
Library of Congress Cataloging-in-Publication Data is available upon request.
ISBN 978-1-5247-2064-3 (hc)
ISBN 978-1-5247-2065-0 (lib. bdg.)
ISBN 978-1-5247-2066-7 (ebook)

The text of this book is set in 15-point Bembo Book.
The illustrations were rendered in Acryla Gouache on illustration board.
Book design by Rachael Cole

PRINTED IN THE UNITED STATES OF AMERICA
10 9 8 7 6 5 4 3 2
First Edition

Random House Children's Books supports the First Amendment and celebrates the right to read.

Sweet Justice

GEORGIA GILMORE AND THE MONTGOMERY BUS BOYCOTT

words by

Mara Rockliff

pictures by Caldecott Honor winner

R. Gregory Christie

RANDOM HOUSE STUDIO NEW YORK

LION

Georgia was cooking when she heard the news.

Mrs. Rosa Parks had been arrested—pulled right off a city bus and thrown in jail because she wouldn't let a white man take her seat.

That was no surprise to Georgia. She had lived her whole life here in Montgomery, Alabama, and she knew there was no justice under segregation.

Segregation was a long, hot summer dragging wishful children past the shady park with the Whites Only sign.

It was the pale pink hands of waitresses serving white businessmen their lunch, as if it wasn't Georgia in the kitchen cooking up Montgomery's best meat loaf and her famous sweet potato pie.

And the city buses! Standing on her aching feet all the way home after a long day's work, with rows and rows of seats up front left empty, just in case a white person got on

But Georgia didn't ride the buses anymore. Not since the day that driver shouted at her to get off the bus and go to the back door, after she'd already paid her ten-cent fare. Before she could get on again, he slammed the doors shut and drove off.

More than a month had passed, and Georgia hadn't stepped onto a city bus. Walking home was even harder on her feet than standing, but she would not give that bus company another dime.

Come Monday, though, she wouldn't have to walk alone. To protest the arrest of Mrs. Parks, the radio was urging everyone to stay off city buses for one day: December 5, 1955. A boycott! Something was cooking in Montgomery, and not just Georgia's black-eyed peas.

Monday morning turned up cold and gray, fixing to rain. A hard day to ask folks to walk. But as the empty buses started rolling by, Georgia could see that it would be a fine day after all. A very fine cold, rainy day indeed.

BAPTIST CHURCH
903

That evening, Georgia headed over to a meeting at the Holt Street Baptist Church. Seemed like all of Montgomery was there—upstairs and downstairs, spilling out onto the streets for blocks around. Mrs. Parks herself could barely manage to squeeze through the crowd.

A young minister named Dr. Martin Luther King Jr. stood up to speak. Georgia knew him. He lived on South Jackson Street, a short walk from her house on Dericote. When he had special company, he'd hire Georgia to fry up a batch of crispy chicken for his guests.

Tonight, Dr. King wasn't talking about chicken. He was talking about justice.

He said, "My friends, there comes a time when people get tired of being trampled over by the iron feet of oppression."

He said, "The great glory of American democracy is the right to protest for right."

He said, "We are determined here in Montgomery to work and fight until justice runs down like water, and righteousness like a mighty stream."

Everyone agreed: the boycott must go on.

Walking with others now, walking to make a change, Georgia hardly even felt her tired feet. Still, many people couldn't get to work or school without the bus. Car owners offered rides, but who would pay for all that gasoline?

Georgia and her friends piled up their money—fifty cents from one, a quarter from another. It wouldn't buy a lot of gas. But if Georgia used it to buy chicken, she could whip up some mouthwatering sandwiches to sell at the next Monday meeting at the church.

It turned out that Dr. King was not the only one who couldn't resist Georgia's crispy chicken. As fast as Georgia's basket emptied out, the collection plate filled up.

Sandwiches were just the start. Georgia moved on to dinners, and then cakes and pies.

Soon she was selling them all over town.

Georgia knew that many people wanted to help out, but they were scared. They could be threatened by their neighbors, fired from their jobs—or worse.

So Georgia called her friends the Club from Nowhere, and she kept their help a secret. Nobody would know who slipped her a few dollars or dropped off a chocolate cake.

Monday evenings at the church, grim-faced policemen sat up front, taking down names. Georgia didn't pay them any mind. Shouts and stomping shook the pews as she presented all the money she had raised—"from nowhere."

The empty buses made city officials hotter than Georgia's collard greens with pepper sauce. They didn't like to lose those bus fares, but they didn't want to change.

They sent out the police to ticket anyone who gave the boycotters a lift. People were arrested just for standing on the corner, waiting for a ride. Georgia made more pound cakes and banana puddings to help pay their fines.

Then, in February, they arrested Dr. King. It was against the law, they said, to organize a boycott that had no "just cause."

No just cause?

Georgia couldn't fight this battle from her kitchen. So she put on her Sunday suit and went down to the courthouse for the trial.

Georgia told the judge about the bus driver who took her dime and then drove off. What kind of way was that to treat a paying customer? Bus riders might look different, Georgia pointed out, but everybody's money was the same.

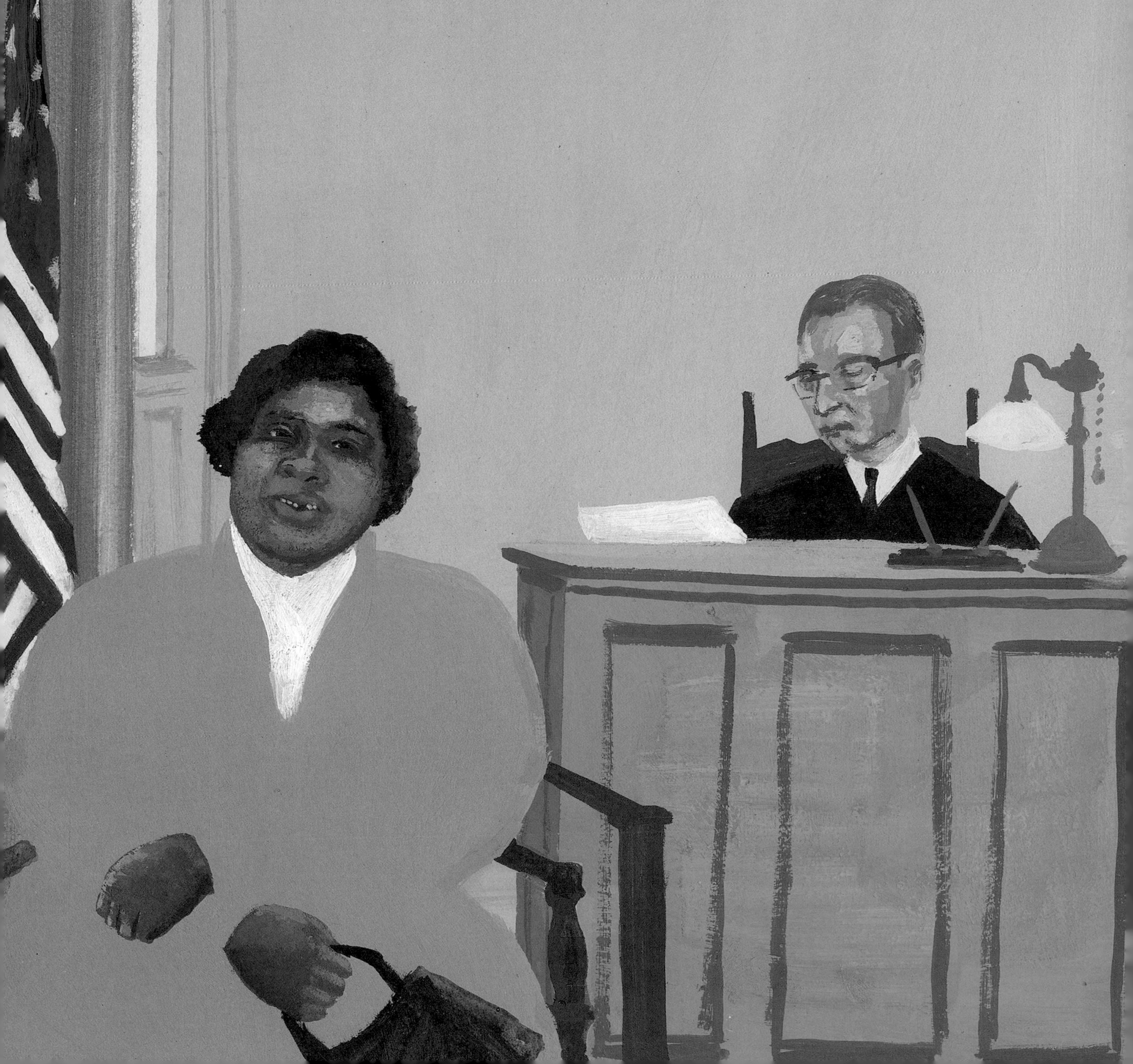

Georgia's testimony didn't save Dr. King from an unfair verdict: guilty. But the journalists who packed the courtroom took her words, and other details of the trial, to the world. Suddenly, everyone was talking about the struggle for justice in Montgomery. Everybody knew the name of Dr. Martin Luther King.

And Georgia?

After she was quoted in the papers, she was fired from her job.

Dr. King encouraged Georgia to start working for herself, selling lunches out of her own kitchen on Dericote Street. He even gave her money to buy pots and pans.

At Georgia's place, everyone crowded happily around her table, or squeezed side by side onto a couch. And if they couldn't find a seat—well, even standing up, they found the spare ribs and the stuffed bell peppers tasted just as good.

Georgia's wasn't just a place for eating, though. It was a place to meet and talk and plan. Spring had come, but still city officials wouldn't budge. Fortified by Georgia's sweet potato pie, the boycotters were determined to stay off the bus.

Summer heated up, frying the sidewalks like a pork chop sizzling in one of Georgia's pans. The boycotters trudged on.

Fall passed, with cold mornings and the comfort of hot rolls from Georgia's oven. The boycotters plodded on.

Georgia was cooking when she heard the news.

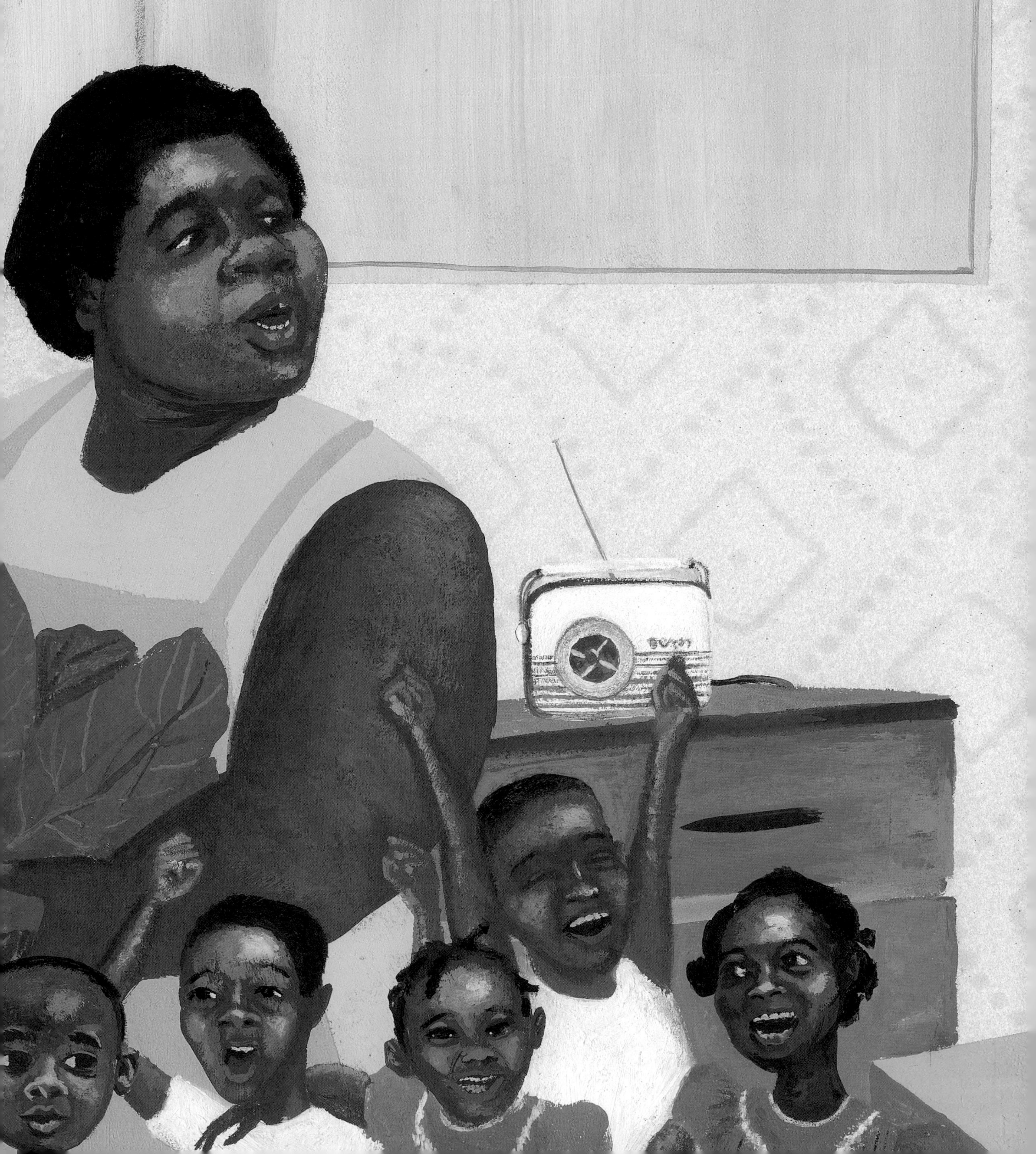

The Supreme Court of the United States had ruled that segregated buses were unconstitutional. On December 20, 1956, Montgomery was ordered to desegregate its buses. From now on, all riders could sit anywhere they liked.

After more than a year, the boycotters had won.

Now, some folks in Montgomery said they had never tasted anything like Georgia's chicken. Some declared there could be nothing more delicious than her pie.

But that night, they tasted justice.

And nothing else Georgia cooked up would ever taste so sweet.

AFTER THE BOYCOTT

Years later, Georgia Gilmore remembered that last meeting at the Holt Street Baptist Church, saying, "Weary feet and weary souls were lightened. It was such a night. We didn't have to walk no more."

The Montgomery bus boycott lasted from December 5, 1955, to December 20, 1956. Although it ended segregation on the city buses, it did not end all legalized racial discrimination. Restaurants, hotels, movie theaters, schools, parks, and other public places were still segregated in Montgomery and elsewhere in the South.

In 1957, Georgia's teenage son Mark was arrested and beaten for taking a shortcut across a whites-only park. After a federal class-action lawsuit (Gilmore v. City of Montgomery), Montgomery was ordered to desegregate its parks. Rather than comply, the city closed down every public park. Bulldozers pushed dirt into the swimming pools. When the public library was also ordered to desegregate, the city took out all the chairs.

Despite such acts, the movement grew and spread. Nine Black teenagers braved angry mobs to integrate a high school in Little Rock, Arkansas. Students organized sit-ins at segregated lunch counters across the South. In 1963, more than 250,000 people joined the March on Washington for Jobs and Freedom, where they heard Martin Luther King Jr. give his now-legendary "I Have a Dream" speech.

Georgia's home at 405 Dericote Street (she later moved to 453) remained a center of the civil rights movement for years. Dr. King often brought important leaders there for secret meetings, including fellow activist Ralph Abernathy, Senator Bobby Kennedy, and two presidents, John F. Kennedy and Lyndon B. Johnson. (While King loved Georgia's pineapple upside-down cake, JFK reportedly favored her sweet potato pie.)

AP Images

Georgia Gilmore, 1956

The day she died, Georgia was cooking up a big batch of fried chicken and potato salad for the twenty-fifth anniversary of the 1965 march for voting rights from Selma, Alabama, to Montgomery. After the funeral, friends and relatives brought food to her house, but no one ate any of it until the food that she herself had cooked was gone. Georgia's cooking was the best.

A big woman with a big personality and an even bigger heart, Georgia Gilmore (1920–1990) was known equally for her kindness and her courage. She was born in Montgomery, Alabama, and lived there her whole life. She worked hard cleaning houses, cooking, and delivering babies as a midwife in the Black community. She also raised six children, plus a younger sister and a niece.

Today, everyone has heard of the Reverend Dr. Martin Luther King Jr. and Rosa Parks. But the fight for justice and equality has never been the work of a few famous people. It was—and is—the work of thousands of courageous and persistent individuals like Georgia Gilmore. Although they might be in the "Club from Nowhere," they are heroes too.

"You cannot be afraid if you want to accomplish anything.
You got to have the willing, the spirit, and above all, you got to have the get-up."
—Georgia Gilmore

AUTHOR'S NOTE ON SOURCES

Sweet Justice is nonfiction, which means nothing in the book is "just made up." How do I know that Georgia Gilmore made banana pudding? Her son said so in an interview. How can I be sure that she wore a suit to the trial? Her photo was in the newspapers. What makes me think that it was cold and rainy on the first day of the boycott? One of the main organizers, Jo Ann Robinson, recalled that weather in her memoir—but just to be certain, I also checked a weather history site.

Of course, not every source is trustworthy, and any source may include a few mistakes. And finding a second source for a statement is no guarantee it's true. Often, an error from one source is repeated in another. As a researcher, I've learned to keep a sharp eye out for inconsistencies, use common sense, and keep on digging till I'm satisfied.

One book I read said that Georgia "moved to Montgomery in 1920." This puzzled me, because the records say that she was born in 1920 . . . in Montgomery. Then I read the transcript of her testimony at the trial of Martin Luther King. The first question she was asked was "How long have you been a resident of the City of Montgomery?" She said, "I don't know how long. I came here in 1920." Reading that, I realized what she really meant was "Don't ask me my age!"

Even the most solid-looking sources can be wrong—such as the historical marker that has stood for decades outside Georgia Gilmore's house and that contains a number of mistakes. Visit mararockliff.com/challenge to see if you can find them all yourself!

SOURCES

Barnett, Bernice McNair. "Invisible Southern Black Women Leaders in the Civil Rights Movement." *Gender & Society,* June 1993.

"Browder v. Gayle, 352 U.S. 903 (1956)," kinginstitute.stanford.edu/encyclopedia/browder-v-gayle-352-us-903.

Chappell, David L. *Inside Agitators: White Southerners in the Civil Rights Movement.* Baltimore: Johns Hopkins University Press, 1994.

Cunningham, Evelyn. "Dull Moments Were Few at Pastor King's Trial." *The Pittsburgh Courier,* March 31, 1956.

Edge, John T. "The Welcome Table." *Oxford American,* January–February 2000.

Garrow, David J., ed. *The Montgomery Bus Boycott and the Women Who Started It: The Memoir of Jo Ann Gibson Robinson.* Knoxville: University of Tennessee Press, 1987.

"Georgia Theresa Gilmore." Ancestry.com.

Gilmore, Georgia. Interview conducted by Blackside Inc. on February 17, 1986, for the PBS documentary *Eyes on the Prize: America's Civil Rights Years, 1954–1965.* Washington University Libraries, Film and Media Archive, Henry Hampton Collection.

Greenhaw, Wayne. *Fighting the Devil in Dixie: How Civil Rights Activists Took On the Ku Klux Klan in Alabama.* Chicago: Lawrence Hill Books, 2011.

Hampton, Henry, and Steve Fayer, with Sarah Flynn. *Voices of Freedom: An Oral History of the Civil Rights Movement from the 1950s Through the 1980s.* New York: Bantam Books, 1990.

Ingram, Bob. "Supreme Court Outlaws Bus Segregation." *The Montgomery Advertiser,* November 14, 1956.

Jarrett, Vernon. "Raised Funds for Blacks: 'Club from Nowhere' Paid Way of Boycott." *Chicago Tribune,* December 4, 1975.

King, Martin Luther, Jr. *Stride Toward Freedom: The Montgomery Story.* Boston: Beacon Press, 2010. (Originally published 1958.)

"The Kitchen of a Civil Rights Hero." National Public Radio, *News & Notes,* July 4, 2005. Transcript of National Public Radio show. npr.org/transcripts/4728761.

Mastin, Frank, Jr. "'Big Momma' Gilmore's Cooking Fueled Movement." *Montgomery Advertiser,* January 19, 1997.

"MIA Mass Meeting at Holt Street Baptist Church," kinginstitute.stanford.edu/king-papers/documents/mia-mass-meeting-holt-street-baptist-church. (Source for quotations from Martin Luther King Jr.'s speech.)

Millner, Steven M. "The Montgomery Bus Boycott: A Case Study in the Emergence and Career of a Social Movement." In David J. Garrow, ed., *The Walking City: The Montgomery Bus Boycott, 1955–1956.* New York: Carlson Publishing Series, 1989.

Nadasen, Premilla. *Household Workers Unite: The Untold Story of African American Women Who Built a Movement.* Boston: Beacon Press, 2015.

Nelson, Davia, and Nikki Silva. *Hidden Kitchens: Stories, Recipes, and More from NPR's The Kitchen Sisters.* Emmaus, PA: Rodale Books, 2006.

"Rev. King's Own Story." *Chicago Defender,* March 31, 1956.

Seay, Solomon S., Jr., with Delores R. Boyd. *Jim Crow and Me: Stories from My Life as a Civil Rights Lawyer.* Montgomery: NewSouth Books, 2008.

Shriver, Jerry. "Southern History, as Told Through Its Cuisine." *USA Today,* July 28, 2000.

"Testimony in State of Alabama v. M. L. King, Jr.," kinginstitute.stanford.edu/king-papers/documents/testimony-state-alabama-v-m-l-king-jr.

Trial transcript of State of Alabama v. M. L. King, Jr. Reprinted in Stewart Burns, ed., *Daybreak of Freedom: The Montgomery Bus Boycott.* Chapel Hill: University of North Carolina Press, 1997.

United Press. "Quotes from the News." *Brownwood* (TX) *Bulletin,* March 22, 1956.

wunderground.com/history. (Source for weather history.)

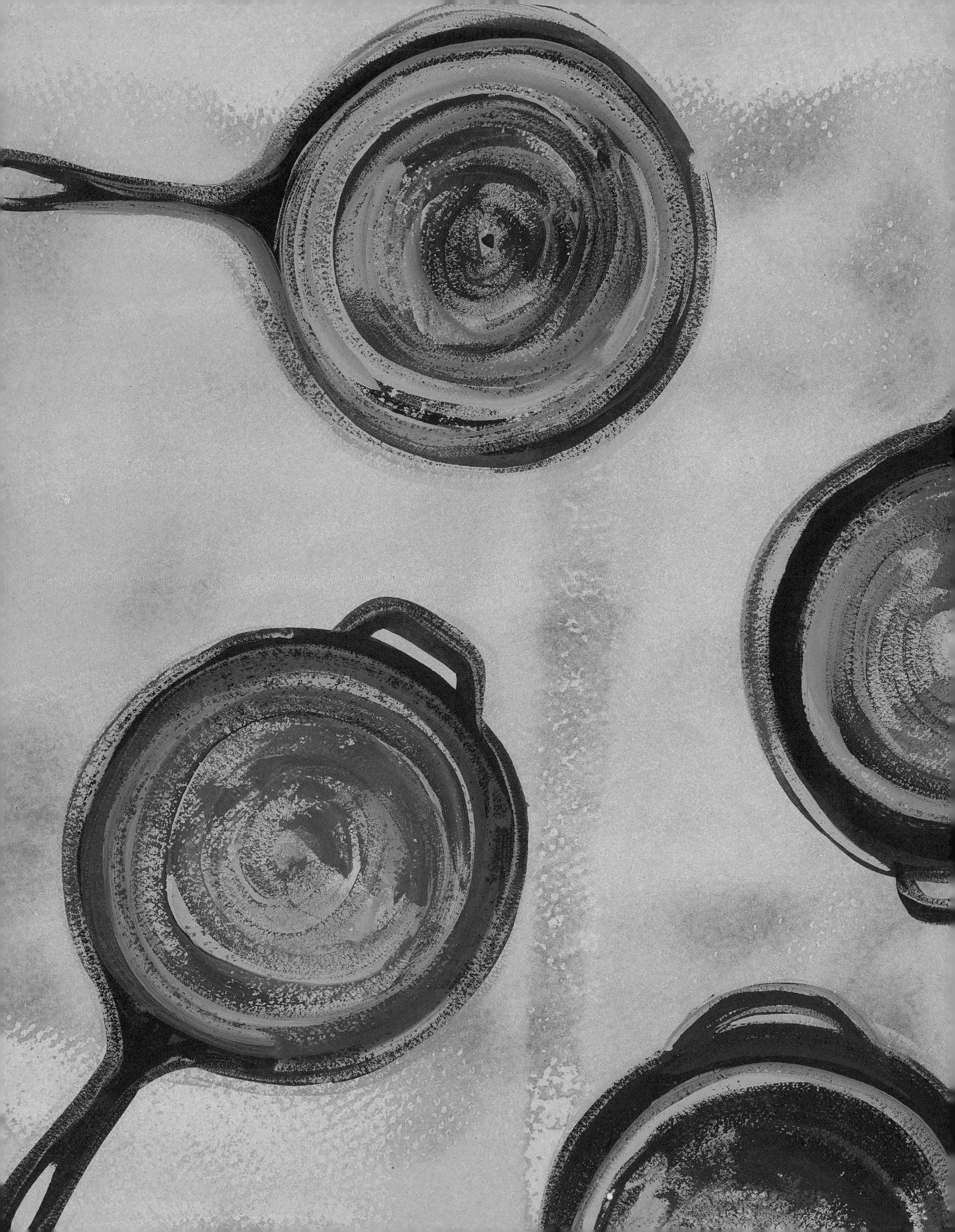